Wild Ozark™ Presents

A DIY Ginseng HABITAT & SITE ASSESSMENT GUIDE

Companion Plants

The mission of Wild Ozark: Bridging the gap between people and the natural world, reminding that we are part of a larger whole, celebrating through stories the imagination that knows all we see is not always all there is.

Cover and interior photography by © Madison Woods

© 2014 by Madison Woods

All rights reserved. No part of this book may be reproduced without written permission from the publisher, except by a reviewer who may quote brief passages or reproduce illustrations in a review with appropriate credits; nor may any part of this book be reproduced, stored in a retrieval system, or transmitted in any form or by any means – electronic, mechanical, photocopying, recording, or other – without written permission from the publisher.

Wild Ozark™

http://www.wildozark.com

Contents

Foreword	*4*
Site Assessment	**5**
Overview	*6*
The Companion Plants	**9**
Trees	*10*
Shrubs	*10*
Ground Cover	*11*
Photos of the Shrubs and Ground Cover	*12*
Is Ginseng Already There?	**29**
Look for anything you think might be ginseng	*30*
Get Down to Ground Level	**34**
Ground & Soil	*35*
Index	*38*

Foreword

This document isn't going to be "about" ginseng. It's about how to find the best places to grow your own virtually-wild or wild-simulated ginseng. It's also about how to find the places on your property where ginseng is likely to already be growing. The only difference between "wild" and "virtually wild" is that the seed was placed by a human in the virtually wild.

So let's hop right to the subject. Get into the woods with your notebook and camera.

You'll need to note some details about your forested locations. Each of the following sections explains what to look for.

SITE ASSESSMENT

Overview

When you find a place you think might work look around. Which direction you are facing? North is ideal. If you are facing west or east, it can work. South-facing is going to be very difficult or impossible without some important circumstances. Some south facing slopes will work if there are dips deep enough to support a moist and cool environment and if the trees present are more than hickory/oak/pine or cedar.

The following photos show a fairly good ginseng growing area in northwest Arkansas on a mostly western-facing slope and bench. A location with older trees, north facing and denser shade would be better. this area shown grows good 'sang in spite of not being perfect.

Figure 1. Looking west-northwest in very early spring, and (next photo) from below looking uphill at the same slope

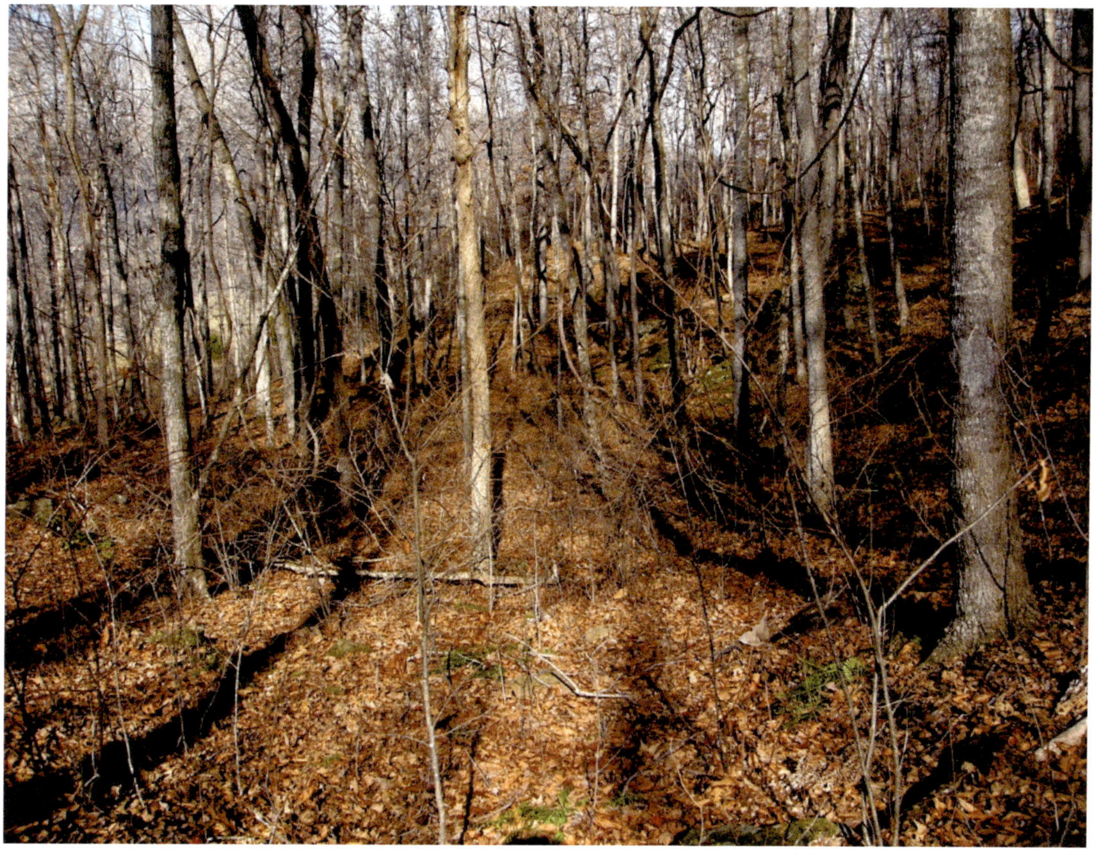

Figure 2. Mid-spring, woods on a western facing bench, facing north in the photo, shows black cohosh in the foreground. Below, later in summer.

The Companion Plants

The other plants that grow in the location is very important in determining whether the site is suitable for ginseng. These certain plants are known as "companion plants" or "indicator plants" because they grow in the kinds of places that ginseng grows. Some of them can tolerate more shade, such as the Christmas and maidenhair ferns. Some of them can endure more sunlight, like black cohosh and mayapple. But when a mix of these plants are present, it usually indicates the proper growing conditions for ginseng.

Trees

If you know what kinds of trees are present, that information is useful. If you don't know the trees, then when spring arrives you'll need to work on identifying them.

The identity of your trees is important. It's okay to have a lot of hickory and oak, but that can't be the only kind there because if it is, the ground-covering leaves will be too heavy for the ginseng plants to push up through in spring. Pine and cedar indicate the area might be too dry, but I've had some luck growing under cedars so it doesn't mean it's impossible. Other trees you really want to see include:

- Maple
- Beech
- Pawpaw
- Redbud
- Poplar
- Dogwood

Shrubs

It's not necessary to have all of the below mentioned shrubs. These plants are known as ginseng companion plants, or indicator plants, because they grow in the same environment that ginseng grows.

In northwestern Arkansas, a very strong indicator is maidenhair fern.

There are some good books to help with identification of plants in the Ozarks. The Peterson's Field Guide to Medicinal Plants, by Duke and Foster, is one.

You'd like to see the following shrubs:

- Black cohosh
- Blue cohosh
- Doll's eyes
- Spicebush
- Witch hazel
- Christmas fern
- Maidenhair fern
- Wild Hydrangea

Ground Cover

Other, smaller plants are also important to look for. The following indicate suitable areas:

- Bloodroot
- Grape or rattlesnake ferns
- Christmas ferns
- Adam and Eve orchid
- Wild ginger
- Trillium
- Giant Solomon's Seal
- False Solomon's Seal
- Jack-in-the-Pulpit
- Goldenseal

Some things you don't want to see too much of:

- poison ivy
- brambles
- cat briars
- grass
- deer berry

Photos of the Shrubs and Ground Cover

The photos on the following pages are of the various companion plants that grow where ginseng grows. Learn to identify your shrubs and plants and look for these when you are out scouting during late spring, summer, and fall.

Figure 3. The flowering top of black cohosh. Also shows spicebush leaves on a branch to the left.

Figure 4. The leaves at the bottom of the black cohosh plant in July during flowering.

Figure 5. Witch hazel. Top shows nuts, bottom just leaves.

Figure 6. Topside of the leaves of a Pawpaw tree, small understory tree. (Below shows from the underside.)

Figure 7. Leaf of an Adam and Eve orchid (above)

Figure 8 .Goldenseal in April

Figure 9. Grape or rattlesnake fern

Figure 10. Grape or Rattlesnake ferns after a frost

Figure 11. Maidenhair fern in April

Figure 12. Maidenhair fern later during summer

Figure 13. Maidenhair fern, shows stems

Figure 14. Mayapple with flower underneath in April

Figure 15. Mayapple leaf as seen from above

Figure 16. Virginia Creeper

Figure 17. Trillium

Figure 18. Wild Ginger

Figure 19. Christmas fern and spicebush

Figure 20. Giant Solomon's Seal

Figure 21. Bloodroot pip

Figure 22. Bloodroot in flower

Figure 23. Mature maple overstory

Figure 24. Jack-in-the-Pulpit

Figure 25. Doll's Eyes w/berries (top) and flower (bottom)

Figure 26. Spicebush (above and below)

Figure 27. Wild Hydrangea

Is Ginseng Already There?

Look for anything you think might be ginseng

Get positive i.d. on it by asking someone who knows. Take a photo of it and send it to me if you don't have anyone nearby who can come see it. I'll be happy to take a look at up to three photos for anyone who's bought this guide. My email address is madison@wildozark.com.

The following photos are of ginseng in various stages. The first photo, however, is of the plant most often mistaken for ginseng. It's Virginia Creeper and until you can tell the difference, it does look a lot alike. Once you know the difference, though, you'll never make the mistake again and wonder how you'd ever gotten the two confused.

Figure 28. Virginia Creeper

It's the uniform size of all five leaves that sets it apart as the lookalike. Ginseng has two very small and three larger leaves.

Figure 29. Ginseng with berries in late July, drought stressed

Figure 30. Closer. Late July, heat and drought stressed with berries

Figure 31. Two-prong ginseng

Figure 32. Two-prong and seedling

Figure 33. Three-prong

Figure 34. Another three-prong

Get Down to Ground Level

Ground & Soil

When you walk into a forest that will support ginseng, it feels cooler. The shade is dense and the ground underneath the leaves is moist. Possibly there are springs on the hills, but not in the precise spots where the planting or growing is going to be done.

When you rake the leaves away, the soil is loamy, dark and crumbly. If you bring it to a laboratory to be tested, the pH will be low and the calcium levels will be high, humus (organic matter) will be high. That's the ideal soil in the ideal place. At the very least it should be dark, moist and crumbly. You'll see the white strings of fungi threading through it and leaves that are decomposing.

Your soil structure is the next thing to look for after the lay, aspect and companion plants. We don't till in the forest at Wild Ozark because the micorrhizal life in the soil is so important for many things to grow well. For example, the grape and rattlesnake ferns depend on certain fungi. They have a symbiotic relationship with it, and cannot grow for long without it. This is why transplanting of that plant doesn't usually work very well unless some of the surrounding native soil is taken with it. The soil life is important to everything in the forest. When tilling is performed, it kills a lot of the microbial and fungal life by exposing it to sunlight and air. The forest is a fragile environment, a habitat perfectly maintained for the plants and animals that grow and live there if man doesn't interfere too drastically. By introducing ginseng to a suitable environment and harvesting responsibly, your interference will be minimal and positive.

The time to plant is after fall has thoroughly set in and before it starts to freeze. For us here in the Ozarks that means September through December, usually.

Figure 35. The ground after leaves have been raked away, on a western facing slope

Figure 36. Close up of the soil. This shows structure, moisture and humus content. You can see white micorrhizal threads on the leaf underside beneath my thumb.

Good luck with your site assessment and happy seeking, planning and planting! I hope you've found this guidebook informative. Please let me know what you thought by leaving a review at the product page where you bought this copy. Thank you!

Wild Ozark™
Madison Woods
http://www.wildozark.com

Index

Adam and Eve orchid 11, 16

Beech 10

black cohosh 8, 13, 14

Black cohosh 11

Bloodroot 11, 24

Blue cohosh 11

brambles 12

cat briars 12

Christmas fern 11, 23

Christmas ferns 11

companion plants 10, 12, 35

deer berry 12

Dogwood 10

Doll's eyes 11

Doll's Eyes 26

False Solomon's Seal 11

Giant Solomon's Seal 11, 23

Goldenseal 11, 16

Grape or rattlesnake ferns 11

grass 12

Ground Cover 3, 11

indicator plants 10

Jack-in-the-Pulpit 11, 25

Maidenhair fern 11, 19, 20

maple 25

Maple 10

Mayapple 20, 21

Overview, site 6

Pawpaw 10, 15

Photos of the Shrubs and Ground Cover 12

poison ivy 12

Poplar 10

Redbud 10

Shrubs 3, 10, 12

Site Assessment 5

Spicebush 11, 27

The Companion Plants 9

Trees 10

Trillium 11, 22

Virginia Creeper 21, 30

virtually wild 4

Wild ginger 11

Wild Ginger 22

Wild Hydrangea 11, 28

Witch hazel 11, 14

Made in the USA
Middletown, DE
22 January 2019